Higher

English

Leckie×Leckie

First exam published in 2002.
Published by Leckie & Leckie, 8 Whitehill Terrace, St. Andrews, Scotland KY16 8RN tel: 01334 475656 fax: 01334 477392
enquiries@leckieandleckie.co.uk www.leckieandleckie.co.uk

ISBN 1-84372-339-5

A CIP Catalogue record for this book is available from the British Library.

Printed in Scotland by Scotprint.

Leckie & Leckie is a division of Granada Learning Limited, part of ITV plc.

Acknowledgements

Leckie & Leckie is grateful to the copyright holders, as credited at the back of the book, for permission to use their material.
Every effort has been made to trace the copyright holders and to obtain their permission for the use of copyright material.
Leckie & Leckie will gladly receive information enabling them to rectify any error or omission in subsequent editions.

[BLANK PAGE]

X039/301

NATIONAL	THURSDAY, 16 MAY	**ENGLISH AND**
QUALIFICATIONS	9.00 AM – 10.30 AM	**COMMUNICATION**
2002		HIGHER
		Close Reading

You should attempt all questions.

The total value of the Paper is 50 marks.

There are TWO passages and questions.

Read both passages carefully and then answer all the questions which follow. **Use your own words whenever possible and particularly when you are instructed to do so.**

You should read each passage to:

understand what the authors are saying about music (**Understanding—U**);

analyse their choices of language, imagery and structures to recognise how they convey their points of view and contribute to the impact of the passages (**Analysis—A**);

evaluate how effectively each writer has achieved his purpose (**Evaluation—E**).

A code letter (U, A, E) is used alongside each question to give some indication of the skills being assessed. The number of marks attached to each question will give some indication of the length of answer required.

SCOTTISH
QUALIFICATIONS
AUTHORITY

PASSAGE 1

The passage is adapted from Big Bangs—The Story of Five Discoveries that Changed Musical History *by Howard Goodall. In this passage, the writer considers the impact of being able to record music.*

We are sitting at one end of a time corridor, over a thousand years long. We, that is you and I, are trying to concentrate on the dark remoteness at the other end—the Dark Ages of Europe. They, the
5 foreigners at the other end, are almost silent. Whilst we are bathed in light and colour, they are hiding from the harsh glare of the sun in what looks like a cell or a tunnel. To us they seem like children in many ways, with their Nativity stories, ghosts
10 and miracles, their unquestioning beliefs and their Gardens of Eden. If they could see us, they would think us indescribably rich and exotic.

At our end of the corridor there is a musical cacophony, at theirs a profound and disheartening
15 silence. At our end of the corridor there are a thousand different voices demanding to be heard, demanding our attention. Music has become more than a backdrop—it has become a blaring soundtrack for practically every event in our lives,
20 whether we are travelling, eating, shopping, exercising, making love or being cremated. We are even given music to "listen to" in the womb. Knowledge and information overwhelm us. At their cold and gloomy end of the corridor,
25 however, only a trickle of learning and culture survives from classical times, mainly through hearsay and deduction.

They have all but lost the flow of the blood of music. It has become for them a distant,
30 heartbreaking echo, surviving only in the keening lamentation of what will one day be known as "Gregorian" plainsong. This, the mother of our music, inherited rough-edged from the Jews, then smoothed into a musical marble, a last mournful
35 relic of centuries of joyful exuberance, is their solace in the medieval gloom. Every single note of the music of Imperial Rome, in the absence of some form of notation, has been lost. What writing is to language, notation is to music. The survival
40 without notation of something quite so delicate as Gregorian plainsong through hundreds of years of war, invasion and pestilence is nothing short of miraculous.

I am a composer. Not an important one, but one
45 who feels nevertheless some kind of ancient, almost mystical gratitude to a humble monk, at the other end of this millennial corridor. Guido Monaco, Guido "the monk", was a jobbing musical director at a cathedral church in what is
50 now called Tuscany in the early years of the eleventh century. He was charged with the task of teaching the choristers the chants which formed the backbone of the worship of that period. To my mind, Guido is no less important than Beethoven

or Presley, Wagner or the Beatles. He is the father 55
and facilitator of every note they wrote. He gave us
our system of musical notation. Guido taught us
how we might write our music down. His
solution—worried out of a bewildering chaos of
possibilities, like precious metal from ore—has 60
served us unswervingly for a thousand years. I am
peering into his empty room, his silent almost
music-less world at the place and time of the birth
of recorded music in Western Europe.

Our gaze now shifts much nearer in the time 65
corridor—to the invention of recorded sound.
Though the early gramophone came into being in
the 1870s as a result of the desire to record and
reproduce speech, very soon its principal, almost
monogamous marriage was with music. Thomas 70
Alva Edison's invention of recorded sound
unleashed on the twentieth century a massive
amount of music in a multitude of forms; it gave
music wings to cross the planet. Before the
gramophone age, people heard a particular piece of 75
orchestral music maybe once or twice a *decade*.
Now anything can be listened to, instantly, at the
flick of a switch, the drop of a needle or the aiming
of a laser. 150 years ago the very slowness of
making a notated score of a piece of music meant 80
that the creator had to live with it and think about it
for a period of time before it was released to the
world. Now a recording can be made
instantaneously, even at the point of creation.
Where once a catchy, impulsive melody made up 85
on the spot and enjoyed for the evening would die
the next morning, never to be heard again, now
everything can be captured for posterity. And in
addition, where once musicians lived and died on
their live performance, now editing allows them to 90
relive and redo their mistakes and wobbles as many
times as they like.

The ability to record sound has had a profound,
irreversible effect on music and what we as
listeners expect from it. A battle has been created 95
between the concept of music as a living,
breathing, organic "condition", ceaselessly
reinventing and reprocessing itself, never static,
never finished, and the concept of music as a
perfect thing, frozen in time like a painting, 100
sculpture, poem or building. At our music-filled
end of the time corridor, have we come to love the
perfect copy a little too much? Are we more at ease
with the reproduction than the genuine live
experience, warts and all? Has recording spoilt us 105
and numbed us to the excitement and drama of the
Real Thing?

PASSAGE 2

The passage is adapted from Lost in Music *by Giles Smith. It is 1972 and the author's two older brothers, Simon and Jeremy, take him (at the age of ten) to see the first live performance of* **Relic**, *the band in which they are drummer and lead guitarist.*

Odd, this business of going out to "see" a band. My parents, when they were younger, would probably have talked about going to hear a band or going to dance to one, and would not have recognised or
5 understood the ritual that evolved with rock: clumps of people solemnly gathering to face the stage.

Lexden Church Hall was a typical modern municipal amenity: orange and green curtains, a
10 squeaky floor and a faint smell of hospitals. To encourage an atmosphere, most of the lights were off. Eventually, a light came on, revealing Jeremy, stamping on a distortion pedal and churning out a monstrous riff, dimly discernible as the opening to
15 "Paranoid" by Black Sabbath.
BLAN, BLAN, BLAN, DIDDLE-DIDDLE-DIDDLE-DIDDLE
BLAN, BLAN, BLAN, DIDDLE-DIDDLE-DIDDLE-DIDDLE
20 Then some more lights came on and the whole band piled in.

I had stood up when the curtains parted but was nearly forced to sit down again by a sickening combination of excitement and fear, which I was to
25 re-experience not long after this at Ipswich stock car stadium, watching a friend of the family compete in a hot-rod race.

Relic crashed through "Long Train Running" by the Doobie Brothers. They thundered into
30 "Locomotive Breath" by Jethro Tull. The evening offered more than a bit part for Fred the roadie. He scuttled on, two minutes in and every three minutes thereafter, bent over at the waist in approved roadie style, to carry out running repairs on the fatigued
35 metal of Simon's drum kit, nobly ducking the bits of splintered drumstick and the hot cymbal shards as he worked.

No one had the confidence to move around during the songs, except the singer, who had confidence to
40 spare. He wore a body-hugging scoop-necked T-shirt and a pair of white trousers as tight in the groin as they were loose at the ankles. He seemed to have learned by heart the *Bumper Book of Mike-stand Manoeuvres*. He lifted its circular weighted
45 base off the floor and toted the stand like a barge pole, in the manner of Rod Stewart; he hopped across the boards, towing it behind him; he forced it down towards the stage in an aggressive tango; he howled into the microphone and then thrust it away
50 to arm's length. Only the low ceiling prevented him from slinging the thing skywards. During instrumental passages, he maintained his place at centre stage, mouth open, nostrils flared, shaking his long blond hair, clapping in time, posturing
55 madly. It was an utterly commanding performance—the performance of a man who knew exactly whose show it was. Accordingly, shortly after this gig, the band voted to replace him with someone much calmer, who came on in a nine-foot
60 scarf and mostly stood at the mike smoking.

At five-second intervals, I glanced down the hall to see what effect all this was having on the audience. It was having very little. The place was about a quarter full. But there were three or four girls at the
65 front watching intently. They looked on gooey-eyed at this frank display of white loon pants and cheap electric guitars.

Near the end of **Relic's** allotted twenty minutes, Simon closed "Honky Tonk Women" with a
70 magnificent final flourish. Sadly there was still a verse to go. Everybody else, catching the imperative force of that last, juddering drum figure, had come to a halt with him. There was a pause, probably only a couple of seconds long, but
75 suddenly time felt heavy as lead. **Relic** exchanged bewildered looks. I felt as if I was about to throw up. But then, like the cavalry regrouping, they set off once more, ground their way back up to speed, beat a path through the final verse and ended again,
80 Simon's flourish sounding a little more sheepish this time. After that, they were gone. And no encores.

I lay in bed that night with singed ears. With hindsight, it has occurred to me that **Relic** were
85 really, by default, Colchester's first punk band, breathtakingly meritless. But I didn't think about that then. I thought about the noise, the lights, the leaping around. I thought about the gooey-eyed girls. I thought I could see a way forward.

Questions on Passage 1

Marks   Code

1. Consider lines 1–12.

  (a) Using your own words as far as possible, identify **two** ways in which the world of "the Dark Ages of Europe" (line 4) was different from ours.   2   U

  (b) Show how the writer's word choice in these lines illuminates any **two** aspects of either our world or theirs.   4   A

2. (a) "At our end . . . silence." (lines 13–15)

     Using your own words as far as possible, explain the meaning of this sentence.   2   U

  (b) Show how the writer's sentence structure and imagery emphasise the contrasting musical environments of people in the Dark Ages and people today. You should refer to lines 13–27 in your answer.   4   A

3. Consider lines 28–43.

  (a) Explain briefly the importance of Gregorian plainsong:

    (i) in the lives of the Dark Ages people;   1   U

    (ii) to the music of our times.   1   U

  (b) Explain briefly **two** reasons why the survival of Gregorian plainsong is "nothing short of miraculous" (lines 42–43).   2   U

4. Consider lines 44–64.

  (a) Explain why, according to the writer, people today should feel gratitude towards Guido Monaco.   2   U

  (b) Show how the writer's language highlights the importance of what Guido Monaco did. You should refer to **one** technique in your answer.   2   A

5. Consider lines 65–92.

   Using your own words as far as possible, identify **five** benefits the gramophone has brought to the world of music.   5   U

6. (a) Using your own words as far as possible, explain the "battle" (line 95) described by the writer in lines 93–107.   2   U

  (b) In lines 101–107, the writer poses three questions. What do you think his answer would be to each of these questions? Justify your view in each case by referring briefly to the language of each question.   3   A

(30)

Questions on Passage 2

7. Explain the significance of the word "ritual" (line 5) in the context of lines 1–7.   2   U

8. Consider lines 8–37.

   Show how the writer conveys his feelings about the whole experience described in these lines. In your answer you may refer to tone, point of view, onomatopoeia, imagery, or any other appropriate language feature.   4   A

9. Consider lines 38–60.

  (a) Which contributes more to the writer's presentation of the singer: **word choice** or **sentence structure**? Justify your choice by referring closely to both of these features.   4   A/E

  (b) Identify the tone of lines 57–60 ("Accordingly . . . at the mike smoking").   1   A

10. "breathtakingly meritless" (line 86)

   By referring to lines 61–82, explain fully what justification the writer has for making this comment about **Relic**.   3   U

(14)

Question on both Passages

11. Which passage did you find more stimulating?

   In your answer you should refer to the styles and to the ideas of both passages. You may make reference to material you have used in earlier answers.   6   E

[END OF QUESTION PAPER]

Total (50)

X039/302

NATIONAL
QUALIFICATIONS
2002

THURSDAY, 16 MAY
10.50 AM – 12.20 PM

ENGLISH AND COMMUNICATION

HIGHER

Analysis and Appreciation

There are **two parts** to this paper and you should attempt both parts.

Part 1 (Textual Analysis) is worth 30 marks.

In Part 2 (Critical Essay), you should attempt **one** question only, taken from any of the Sections A–D.

Your answer to Part 2 should begin on a fresh page.

Each question in Part 2 is worth 30 marks.

NB You must not use, in Part 2 of this paper, the same text(s) as you have used in your Specialist Study.

PIB X039/302 6/38170

SCOTTISH
QUALIFICATIONS
AUTHORITY

PART 1—TEXTUAL ANALYSIS

Read the following passage and answer the questions which follow.

You are reminded that this part of the paper tests your ability to understand, analyse and evaluate the text.

The number of marks attached to each question will give some indication of the length of answer required.

You should spend about 45 minutes on this part of the paper.

The following passage is about the writer's visit to see "The Jaguar Throne" which is inside a pyramid at Chichen Itza, a site of ancient Mayan civilisation in Mexico.

The Jaguar Throne

We're standing in line to see the Jaguar Throne. It's almost Christmas now and everything is crowded, including the monasteries converted to ten-dollar-a-room hotels and the washrooms
5 crammed with feet, in pastel sandals and the smell of orange peels and other things, and the crumbling hilltop temples with their inner walls luxuriant with graffiti, but this is the last chance we may ever have. Who knows when we'll be
10 passing this way again?

The Jaguar Throne is embedded in a pyramid. First you go through a narrow tunnel entered at ground level, a tunnel so narrow your shoulders touch each side, the old stone unpleasantly
15 damp, with a skin on it like the skin on a stagnant pond. There is only one passageway. Those who have already seen the Jaguar Throne push past us on the way back, squeezing us against the skin of the wall, in their hurry to
20 reach the outside air again. Eagerly we scan their faces: was it worth it?

There are a few small lightbulbs strung along the ceiling, a wire festooned between them. The ceiling itself is getting lower. The air is moist
25 and dead. The line inches forward. Ahead of us there are backs, the necks sunburned, the shirts and dresses ringed with sweat beneath the arms. Nobody says anything, though the heavy air seems full of whispers. Ahead of us, up some
30 steps, around corners unseen, the Jaguar Throne crouches in a square cubicle, its ruby eyes glowing, its teeth vivid, its meaning lost. Who used it last, what was it for, why was it kept here, out of sight in the darkness?

The line of people moves forward into the 35 absence of light. There must have been processions once, flames carried, dimming in the lack of oxygen, men in masks, willing or not. The Jaguar Throne was not always a curiosity, something to see at Christmas. Once there were 40 gods who needed propitiation. Once they played a game here, in an outside court, with stone rings set into the walls. If your team lost they cut off your head. That's what the carving is, the body of a man with a fountain in place of 45 the head: the blessed loser, making it rain. Metaphor can be dangerous. Not everyone wants to see the Jaguar Throne but some see it anyway.

Ahead of us a woman screams. Panic runs 50 through the line, you can feel it jumping from body to body, there's a surge backwards: in a minute we'll be stampeded, crushed. Then comes the rumour, the whisper: it was only a spider. We're caught anyway, the tunnel's 55 jammed, we can't move, we stand in the dead air listening to our hearts, and now we know the answer: the Jaguar Throne is kept in here so it can't get out.

Margaret Atwood

QUESTIONS

Marks

1. (*a*) What mood or atmosphere do you think is created in lines 1–10?   1

   (*b*) Show how this mood or atmosphere is created. In your answer you should refer to at least two techniques such as word choice, tone, sentence structure.   4

2. Read lines 11–21.

   (*a*) Explain fully how the language of these lines makes the experience described seem unpleasant.   4

   (*b*) Show how effective you find the last sentence "Eagerly we scan . . ." as a conclusion to the paragraph.   2

3. (*a*) Select one detail from the description in lines 22–29 ("There are a few . . . full of whispers.") and show how it creates an oppressive or a claustrophobic mood.   2

   (*b*) In what ways do sentence structure and imagery in lines 29–34 contribute to the mysterious nature of the Jaguar Throne?   4

4. (*a*) By referring to lines 35–49, briefly describe three key features of the rituals associated with the Jaguar Throne. Use your own words as far as possible.   3

   (*b*) Explain what you think "Metaphor can be dangerous" (line 47) means in the context of lines 43–46.   2

5. Explain how the language of the final paragraph (lines 50–59) develops the crowd's sense of panic. In your answer you should refer to techniques such as sentence structure, imagery, punctuation, word-choice . . .   4

6. "the Jaguar Throne is kept in here so it can't get out." (lines 58–59)

   By referring to the passage as a whole, explain why you think the narrator draws this conclusion about the significance of the Jaguar Throne.   4

   (30)

[Turn over for PART 2—CRITICAL ESSAY

PART 2—CRITICAL ESSAY

Attempt ONE question only, taken from any of the Sections A to D. Write the number of the question you attempt in the margin of your answer book.

In all Sections you may use Scottish texts.

You must not use the extract from the Textual Analysis part of the paper as the subject of your Critical Essay.

You are reminded that the quality of your writing and its accuracy are important in this paper as is the relevance of your answer to the question you have attempted.

You should spend about 45 minutes on this part of the paper.

Begin your answer on a fresh page.

SECTION A—DRAMA

1. Choose a play in which a character struggles with her or his conscience.

   Outline briefly the reasons for the character's dilemma and go on to discuss how successfully the dramatist engages your sympathy for her or him.

   In your answer you must refer closely to the text and to at least two of: characterisation, conflict, theme, resolution, or any other appropriate feature.

2. Choose from a play a scene in which the conflict between two characters is at its most intense.

   Outline briefly the reasons for the conflict and then by examining the scene in detail, show how it gave you a deeper appreciation of the play as a whole.

   In your answer you must refer closely to the text and to at least two of: key scene, dialogue, characterisation, structure, or any other appropriate feature.

3. Choose a play whose main theme concerns one of the following: power, corruption, disillusionment.

   Explain how the dramatist introduces the theme and discuss to what extent you found the way it is explored in the play enhanced your understanding of the theme.

   In your answer you must refer closely to the text and to at least two of: theme, plot, setting, characterisation, or any other appropriate feature.

4. Choose a play in which the main character is at odds with one or more than one of the people around him or her.

   Show how the dramatist makes you aware of the character's situation and discuss to what extent this led to a greater understanding of the concerns of the play.

   In your answer you must refer closely to the text and to at least two of: conflict, characterisation, theme, setting, or any other appropriate feature.

SECTION B—PROSE

(In this Section you may not answer using "The Jaguar Throne" by Margaret Atwood.)

5. Choose a **novel or short story** in which the main character faces a dilemma.

   Outline briefly what the dilemma is and go on to discuss how the character's reaction to it gives you a deeper understanding of the text as a whole.

   In your answer you must refer closely to the text and to at least two of: theme, structure, setting, characterisation, or any other appropriate feature.

6. Choose a **novel** which explores in an effective way a theme which is important to you.

   Explain how the novelist introduces and develops the theme and show to what extent she or he has effectively engaged your interest in it.

   In your answer you must refer closely to the text and to at least two of: theme, structure, setting, symbolism, or any other appropriate feature.

7. Choose a **novel** in which a main character is seen to grow or mature in the course of the story.

   Show how the novelist engages your interest in the character and his or her development.

   In your answer you must refer closely to the text and to at least two of: characterisation, narrative point of view, key incident(s), structure, or any other appropriate feature.

8. Choose a **novel or short story** which has a particularly effective or arresting opening.

   Referring in detail to the opening, discuss to what extent it provides a successful introduction to the text as a whole.

   In your answer you must refer closely to the text and to at least two of: structure, mood, theme, characterisation, or any other appropriate feature.

9. Choose a work of **non-fiction** in which setting in time and/or place is significant.

   Explain why you think the setting is important for your appreciation of the text.

   In your answer you must refer closely to the text and to at least two of: setting, theme, style, descriptive detail, or any other relevant feature.

SECTION C—POETRY

10. Choose a poem in which contrast is used in order to clarify a key idea.

    Examine in detail the poet's use of contrast and show how it was effective in clarifying this key idea.

    In your answer you must refer closely to the text and to at least two of: theme, structure, imagery, sound, or any other appropriate feature.

11. Choose a poet who reflects on the power, the beauty or the threat of the natural world.

    Referring to one or more poems, show how effectively you think the poet explores her or his main idea(s).

    In your answer you must refer closely to the text and to at least two of: mood, imagery, symbolism, sound, or any other appropriate feature.

12. Choose a poem which explores one of the following: freedom, friendship, happiness.

    Discuss to what extent the poem successfully engages your interest in this main idea.

    In your answer you must refer closely to the text and to at least two of: theme, tone, word choice, rhythm, or any other appropriate feature.

13. Choose a poem which presents a character who provokes you to contempt or anger or irritation.

    Show how the poet arouses this response from you and discuss how important it is to the overall impact of the poem.

    In your answer you must refer closely to the text and to at least two of: tone, characterisation, verse form, point of view, or any other appropriate feature.

SECTION D—MASS MEDIA

14. Choose a film which has a particularly effective or arresting opening.

    Referring in detail to the opening, discuss to what extent it provides a successful introduction to the text as a whole.

    In your answer you must refer closely to the text and to at least two of: aspects of mise-en-scène, structure, editing, soundtrack, or any other appropriate feature.

15. Choose from a film or TV drama* a scene in which the conflict between two characters is at its most intense.

    Outline briefly the reasons for the conflict and then by examining the scene in detail, show how it gave you a deeper appreciation of the text as a whole.

    In your answer you must refer closely to the text and to at least two of: key scene, characterisation, dialogue, aspects of mise-en-scène, or any other appropriate feature.

16. Choose a TV drama* in which the character struggles with her or his conscience.

    Outline briefly the reasons for the character's dilemma and go on to discuss how successfully the programme-makers engage your sympathy for her or him.

    In your answer you must refer closely to the text and to at least two of: theme, characterisation, editing, aspects of mise-en-scène, or any other appropriate feature.

17. Choose a film or TV drama* in which setting in time and/or place is significant.

    Explain why you think the setting is important for your appreciation of the text.

    In your answer you must refer closely to the text and to at least two of: setting, aspects of mise-en-scène, theme, soundtrack, or any other appropriate feature.

*"TV drama" may be a single play, series or serial.

[END OF QUESTION PAPER]

[BLANK PAGE]

[C115/SQP215]

NATIONAL
QUALIFICATIONS

Time: 1 hour 30 minutes

ENGLISH
HIGHER
Close Reading
Specimen Question Paper
(for examinations in and after 2003)

Answer all questions.

50 marks are allocated to this paper.

There are TWO passages and questions.

Read both passages carefully and then answer all the questions which follow. **Use your own words whenever possible and particularly when you are instructed to do so.**

You should read each passage to:

understand what the authors are saying about global warming and its effects (**Understanding—U**);

analyse their choices of language, imagery and structures to recognise how they convey their points of view and contribute to the impact of the passages (**Analysis—A**);

evaluate how effectively they have achieved their purposes (**Evaluation—E**).

A code letter (U, A, E) is used alongside each question to give some indication of the skills being assessed. The number of marks attached to each question will give some indication of the length of answer required.

SCOTTISH
QUALIFICATIONS
AUTHORITY

PASSAGE 1

This passage is from an article by journalist Angus Clark and appeared in The Times *newspaper in November 2000 after severe gales and extensive flooding in various parts of England.*

This is a tale of two towns: both modest, yet possessed of a certain civic pride; both nestled at the edge of the ocean, sharing almost exactly the same latitude. In Churchill, Manitoba, in
5 northern Canada, the winter is long, the snow is deep, the sea freezes far and wide as the thermometer falls to minus 50 degrees centigrade. There are only two months a year without snow. When the polar bears emerge from hibernation
10 they gnaw the dustbins in search of scraps. Churchill, in short, is not a place to grow wheat and roses, potatoes and apples. There are no green dairy farms on the tundra shores of Hudson's Bay. In Inverness, on the east coast of Scotland, the
15 winters are very much gentler and shorter. Cold, yes, but not cold enough for skidoos, treble-glazed windows or snowshoes to school. The nearby Black Isle has some of Scotland's richest arable farmland.

20 The enormous difference between the climates of these two towns is due to one thing: the Gulf Stream, which brings tropic-warmed sea from the Gulf of Mexico to the Atlantic coasts of northern Europe. Thanks to the Gulf Stream, on fine
25 summer days people can swim in the sea from the pale golden beaches of the Lofoten Islands in Norway—300 miles north of the Arctic Circle. In coastal gardens beside its warm waters, sub-tropical plants and exotic flowers flourish.

If there were no Gulf Stream, Britain would be as 30 cold as Manitoba. We would probably be able to walk to Germany across the frozen North Sea. Our farmers would be defeated by permafrost but caribou would thrive on the lichens beneath the snow. Dairy herds would not wind o'er the lea, nor 35 would honeysuckle twine about our cottage porches.

The Gulf Stream has not always flowed. As far as scientists can tell, it has stopped quite abruptly in the past—and in as little as a couple of years. Now 40 it seems that global warming is recreating the very same conditions which caused it to stall before, with the potential to plunge the whole of northern Europe into another Ice Age.

Which is a bit ironic as we slosh around in sodden, 45 rainswept towns and villages; as we discuss the extraordinary late autumn and give up hope for a white Christmas. Global warming was going to bring Mediterranean holiday weather to Brighton and vineyards to Argyll, wasn't it? Global 50 warming is the reason why spring-flowering iris and cistus are blooming crazily in November. So how could it turn England's green and rather tepid land into a frozen waste?

PASSAGE 2

The second passage, by James O. Jackson, appeared in Time *magazine also in November 2000.*

Deluges, droughts, fires, landslides, avalanches, gales, tornadoes; is it just our imagination, or is Europe's weather getting worse?

The short answer is yes, the weather is certainly
5 getting worse. The cause is air pollution that pours greenhouse gases such as carbon dioxide and methane into the atmosphere to produce global warming that can alter weather patterns. Whether the specific storms that scythed down trees in Paris
10 last Christmas, drowned the Po Valley last month and battered Britain last week can be attributed to the warming trend is a subject of serious—and contentious—scientific debate. But most climate experts agree that so-called extreme weather
15 events are becoming more frequent, and that the weather world-wide over the coming 100 years will change drastically. The scientists say that even if the world's governments and industries meet international goals on reducing greenhouse
20 gases—which they probably will not—it still won't be enough to prevent severe changes to the world's weather. Their advice to governments, businesses and private citizens about this is grim: get used to it.

A landmark report released last week by a team of 25 27 European climatologists confirms that the trend in global warming may be irreversible, at least over most of the coming century. That, they say, means governments should start planning immediately to adapt to the new extremes of 30 weather that the citizens will face—with bans on building in potential flood plains in the north, for example, and water conservation measures in the south.

That represents a subtle but significant shift 35 in attitude to global warming and some environmentalist campaigners are dismayed at the suggestion that the world should adapt to the warming trend rather than try to halt or reverse it.

Next week at the Hague, representatives of 160 40 countries will gather to assess progress since the

1997 Kyoto Protocol. In that agreement, governments pledged that, by 2012, they would cut greenhouse emissions to 5·2% below 1992 levels. They are far from meeting that goal, and the Hague conference is likely to turn into a wrangle of finger-pointing over who is at fault. Campaigners for drastic cuts in emissions fear that talk of "adapting" rather than "mitigating" will ease political pressures on the big polluters such as the US and Japan.

All this because, says the Intergovernmental Panel on Climate Change, temperatures could rise by as much as 6 degrees centigrade in the 21st century, ten times as fast as temperatures have risen in the last 100 years. Who will want to live in such a world—especially in some of the regions likely to be hardest hit, which happen to include those already the poorest on the planet? Dry areas will get drier, wet areas will get wetter. Africa will suffer in ways that scientists cannot fully predict, but the Sahel will probably become even drier and more prone to drought and famine than it already is. For Europe, it will mean the influx of such pathogens as malaria, dengue fever and encephalitis as warmer weather encourages the northern movement of disease-carrying mosquitoes. Generally, warmer water can more easily harbour cholera and other waterborne diseases which will be more easily spread during frequent floods.

Some argue that the ultimate result of global warming will be a paradoxical but even more catastrophic development: global cooling. As the Arctic ice cap melts, a flow of fresh water into the North Atlantic could disrupt conveyer currents including the Gulf Stream, which is what keeps northern Europe warm. According to Steve Hall, oceanographer at Southampton Oceanography Centre, "One moment we could be basking in a Mediterranean climate and the next icebergs could be floating down the English Channel." It would take just one quarter of 1% more fresh water

flowing into the North Atlantic from melting Arctic glaciers to bring the northwards flow of the Gulf Stream to a halt.

And in August this year, a tremor of apprehension ran through the scientific community when the Russian ice-breaker *Yamal*, on a tourist cruise of the Arctic, muscled its way through unusually thin ice to the North Pole to find itself sailing serenely into an astonishingly clear blue sea. It was the first time the effects of global warming had been seen so far north.

Steve Hall's tongue may have been lodged firmly in cheek while making his prediction, and certainly few scientists believe the English iceberg scenario is likely even a century from now. Some, indeed, question the accuracy of most if not all of such apocalyptic predictions. "The science of climate change is enormously complicated," says Julian Morris, an environmental analyst at London's Institute of Economic Affairs. "The data are inconclusive, contradictory and confusing." Temperature measurements, for example, have been taken for only a relatively short period of time and may be skewed by such factors as urban expansion. The climatological history of the world is long, he says, and man's knowledge of it is short. "Attempting to make clear assessments of what is driving the climate over these much shorter time spans is fraught with difficulty." But the growing consensus is that momentous changes are coming.

Governments may stop finger-pointing and instead join hands; industries may slash short-term profit to permit long-term survival; populations may realise the cost and embrace huge changes in lifestyle. Only an optimist, though, and an uninformed optimist at that, could believe that humankind will succeed in making such radical changes in time to avert the bad weather ahead. So the best advice is to get out the umbrellas and hip boots and head for high ground. Storms are coming; the water is rising. We—and our descendants—will have to learn to live with it.

Questions on Passage 1

Marks Code

1. (a) By referring to lines 1–4, identify four features which make Churchill and Inverness similar. Use your own words as far as possible. 2 U

   (b) In lines 4–19, the writer contrasts the climate of these two towns. Show how the writer's use of language makes Churchill's climate seem more extreme than that of Inverness. 4 A

2. (a) Explain briefly in your own words why the Gulf Stream, as described in lines 20–24, affects the climate of northern Europe. 1 U

   (b) Show how the writer uses contrast in lines 24–37 to illustrate the impact of the Gulf Stream. You should refer to specific words and phrases in your answer. 4 A

3. Consider lines 38–54.

   (a) Explain the meaning of "stall" as it is used in line 42. 1 U

   (b) (i) What is "ironic" (line 45) about the possible effect of global warming on northern Europe? 2 U

      (ii) Show how the writer, in lines 45–54, emphasises this irony. In your answer, you should refer to such features as sentence structure, tone, word choice. 4 A

   (18)

Questions on Passage 2

4. (a) Explain how any one language feature in lines 1–3 helps to make dramatic the opening of the article. 2 A

   (b) Explain, using your own words as far as possible, why the weather is "getting worse". You should refer to lines 4–8 in your answer. 2 U

   (c) Show how the writer uses imagery in lines 8–13 to emphasise the impact of the storms which affected Europe. You should refer to two examples in your answer. 4 A

   (d) Show how the writer helps to clarify his argument in lines 17–24 by using:

      (i) dashes;

      (ii) a colon. 2 A

5. Consider lines 25–39.

   What is the "shift in attitude" (lines 35–36)? 2 U

6. By referring to lines 40–51, explain briefly in your own words two problems which may emerge at the Hague conference. 2 U

7. (a) In lines 52–86, the writer describes the possible effects of global warming. Using your own words as far as possible, outline briefly the main effects on Africa, on Europe, and on the North Atlantic. 5 U

   (b) In the context of global warming, how effective do you find the writer's anecdote about the *Yamal* (lines 87–94)? Justify your answer. 2 E

8. By referring to lines 95–113, give two reasons why the situation might not be as bleak as is being suggested by many of the scientists. Use your own words as far as possible. 2 U

9. To what extent would you agree that the final paragraph (lines 114–125) is an effective conclusion to the article? Justify your answer by referring to such features as ideas, punctuation, tone, imagery, point of view. 3 E

   (26)

Question on both Passages

10. Which of the two writers appears to treat the topic of global warming more effectively? Justify your choice by referring to such features as ideas, tone, use of examples, style. You should refer to both passages in your answer. 6 E

[END OF SPECIMEN QUESTION PAPER]

Total (50)

[C115/SQP215]

NATIONAL
QUALIFICATIONS

Time: 1 hour 30 minutes

ENGLISH
HIGHER
Critical Essay
Specimen Question Paper
(for examinations in and after 2003)

Answer **two** questions.

Each question must be taken from a different section.

Each question in worth 25 marks.

SCOTTISH
QUALIFICATIONS
AUTHORITY

Answer TWO questions from this paper.

Each question must be chosen from a different Section (A–E). You are not allowed to choose two questions from the same Section.

In all Sections you may use Scottish texts.

Write the number of each question in the margin of your answer booklet and begin each essay on a fresh page. You should spend about 45 minutes on each essay.

The following will be assessed:

- **the relevance of your essays to the questions you have chosen**

- **the quality of your writing**

- **the technical accuracy of your writing.**

Each answer is worth up to 25 marks. The total for this paper is 50 marks.

SECTION A—DRAMA

1. Choose a play in which there is a scene dominated by confusion, complications or uncertainties.

   Explain the cause(s) of the confusion, complications or uncertainties, and go on to discuss the importance of the scene to your appreciation of the play as a whole.

   In your answer you must refer closely to the text and to at least two of: structure, dialogue, conflict, theme, or any other appropriate feature.

2. Choose a play in which a character keeps something hidden or pretends to be something she or he is not.

   Explain the reason(s) for the character's behaviour and discuss how it affects your attitude to the character.

   In your answer you must refer closely to the text and to at least two of: characterisation, dramatic irony, theme, soliloquy, or any other appropriate feature.

3. Choose a play whose main theme is made clear early in the action.

   Show how the dramatist introduces the theme and discuss how successfully he or she goes on to develop it.

   In your answer you must refer closely to the text and to at least two of: theme, key scene(s), characterisation, language, or any other appropriate feature.

4. Choose a play in which one scene or moment determines the fate of a main character.

   Explain fully why you think this is the key moment in the character's fortunes.

   In your answer you must refer closely to the text and to at least two of: key scene, characterisation, climax, dialogue, or any other appropriate feature.

SECTION B—PROSE

5. Choose a **novel** which is influenced by the presence of a powerful or overbearing character.

   Show how the novelist creates this impression of the character and discuss to what extent you felt you could sympathise with him or her.

   In your answer you must refer closely to the text and to at least two of: characterisation, narrative technique, language, theme, or any other appropriate feature.

6. Choose a **novel** or **short story** in which a family disagreement plays an important part.

   Explain the circumstances of the disagreement and show how the writer uses it to develop theme and/or character.

   In your answer you must refer closely to the text and to at least two of: theme, setting, plot, characterisation, or any other appropriate feature.

7. Choose a **novel** or **short story** with a dramatic or shocking ending.

   Show how the writer creates the effect and discuss to what extent it added to your appreciation of the text as a whole.

   In your answer you must refer closely to the text and to at least two of: structure, climax, theme, characterisation, or any other appropriate feature.

8. Choose a **novel** in which the novelist makes effective use of symbolism.

   Show how the writer made use of this technique to enhance your appreciation of the text as a whole.

   In your answer you must refer closely to the text and to at least two of: symbolism, theme, imagery, structure, or any other appropriate feature.

9. Choose a **non-fiction text** which introduced you to a new culture.

   Explain how well the writer achieved that introduction.

   In your answer you must refer closely to the text and to at least two of: narrative voice, ideas, setting, structure, use of anecdote or any other appropriate feature.

10. Choose a **non-fiction text** which made you think about an environmental issue.

    Explain briefly what the issue is and at greater length show how the writer's treatment of the issue conveyed her or his point of view.

    In your answer you must refer closely to the text and to at least two of: ideas, point of view, use of evidence, organisation, use of examples or any other appropriate feature.

11. Choose a **non-fiction text** which presented the life story of a particular person.

    Evaluate the techniques the author used to make the biography enjoyable.

    In your answer you must refer closely to the text and to at least two of: narrative voice, language, anecdote, structure, or any other appropriate feature.

SECTION C—POETRY

12. Choose a poem which is light-hearted or playful or not entirely serious.

    Show how the poet makes you aware of the tone, and discuss how effective the use of this tone is in dealing with the subject matter of the poem.

    In your answer you must refer closely to the text and to at least two of: tone, imagery, theme, sound, or any other appropriate feature.

13. Choose two poems on the subject of war or hostility.

    Compare the way the two poems treat the subject, and explain to what extent you find one more effective than the other.

    In your answer you must refer closely to the text and to at least two of: theme, structure, imagery, rhythm and rhyme, or any other appropriate feature.

14. Choose a poem which depicts one of the following: the sea, the night, the countryside, sleep, a dream, travel.

    Show how the poet brings the subject to life for you.

    In your answer you must refer closely to the text and to at least two of: imagery, atmosphere, sound, theme, or any other appropriate feature.

15. Choose a poem which explores loneliness or isolation.

    Show how the poet explores the theme, and discuss to what extent your appreciation of the theme was deepened by the poet's treatment.

    In your answer you must refer closely to the text and to at least two of: theme, mood, imagery, contrast, or any other appropriate feature.

SECTION D—MASS MEDIA

16. Choose a film which has a particularly effective or arresting opening.

    Referring in detail to the opening, discuss to what extent it provides a successful introduction to the text as a whole.

    In your answer you must refer closely to the text and to at least two of: aspects of mise-en-scène, structure, editing, soundtrack, or any other appropriate feature.

17. Choose from a film or TV drama* a scene in which the conflict between two characters is at its most intense.

    Outline briefly the reasons for the conflict and then by examining the scene in detail, show how it gave you a deeper appreciation of the text as a whole.

    In your answer you must refer closely to the text and to at least two of: key scene, characterisation, dialogue, aspects of mise-en-scène, or any other appropriate feature.

18. Choose a TV drama* in which the character struggles with her or his conscience.

    Outline briefly the reasons for the character's dilemma and go on to discuss how successfully the programme-makers engage your sympathy for her or him.

    In your answer you must refer closely to the text and to at least two of: theme, characterisation, editing, aspects of mise-en-scène, or any other appropriate feature.

19. Choose a film or TV drama* in which setting in time and/or place is significant.

    Explain why you think the setting is important for your appreciation of the text.

    In your answer you must refer closely to the text and to at least two of: setting, aspects of mise-en-scène, theme, soundtrack, or any other appropriate feature.

*"TV drama" may be a single play, series or serial.

SECTION E—LANGUAGE

20. Choose an aspect of language which you have investigated within a specific interest group in society.

    Identify the kind of group or groups you investigated, making clear what it was they had in common. Show to what extent the specialist language connected with the interest of the group(s) increased the effectiveness of communication within the group(s).

    You must refer to specific examples, and to at least two language concepts such as jargon, register, technical terminology, abbreviations or any other appropriate concept.

21. Choose an aspect of communication technology, such as TV, e-mail, mobile phone, which has brought about developments in our language in the last decade.

    Explain the nature of the developments you have investigated and evaluate what impact they had on the effectiveness of communication.

    You must refer to specific examples and to at least two language concepts such as jargon, register, orthography or any other appropriate concept.

22. Choose an aspect of spoken language which you have investigated within a particular age group.

    Briefly describe the parameters of your investigation. Show how far the language characteristics of the group you investigated differed from the general population and go on to evaluate the advantages and disadvantages of these differences.

    You must refer to specific examples and to at least two language concepts such as register, dialect, accent, vocabulary or any other appropriate concept.

23. Choose an area of communication in which emotive language is commonly used to influence the reader, viewer or listener.

    Outline the purposes of the communication(s) you have chosen. Go on to analyse the methods used and evaluate the effectiveness of the communication in achieving its purpose.

    You must refer to specific examples and to at least two language concepts such as word choice, tone, presentation, structure, or any other appropriate concept.

[END OF SPECIMEN QUESTION PAPER]

[BLANK PAGE]

[BLANK PAGE]

X115/301

NATIONAL
QUALIFICATIONS
2003

FRIDAY, 16 MAY
9.00 AM – 10.30 AM

ENGLISH
HIGHER
Close Reading

Answer all questions.

50 marks are allocated to this paper.

There are TWO passages and questions.

Read the passages carefully and then answer all the questions which follow. **Use your own words whenever possible and particularly when you are instructed to do so.**

You should read the passages to:

understand what the writers are saying about refugees, asylum seekers, and immigration in general (**Understanding—U**);

analyse their choices of language, imagery and structures to recognise how they convey their points of view and contribute to the impact of the passages (**Analysis—A**);

evaluate how effectively they have achieved their purposes (**Evaluation—E**).

A code letter (U, A, E) is used alongside each question to give some indication of the skills being assessed. The number of marks attached to each question will give some indication of the length of answer required.

SCOTTISH
QUALIFICATIONS
AUTHORITY

©

PASSAGE 1

The first passage is an article in The Herald *newspaper in June 2002. In it, journalist and broadcaster Ruth Wishart offers some thoughts on attitudes to immigration to Scotland.*

CAN BRITAIN AFFORD TO KEEP TALENTED IMMIGRANTS OUT?

If you hail from Glasgow you will have friends or relatives whose roots lie in the Irish Republic. You will have Jewish friends or colleagues whose grandparents, a good number of them Polish or
5 Russian, may have fled persecution in Europe. You will eat in premises run by Italian or French proprietors. It is a diverse cultural heritage enriched now by a large and vibrant Asian population and a smaller but significant Chinese
10 one.

It was not always thus.

The city census of 1831 found 47 Jewish citizens, a community which grew and prospered as it became an integral part of Glasgow's merchant
15 growth. The first Asian immigrants were no more than a few young men, largely from poor and rural backgrounds, whose early employment as door-to-door salesmen gave no hint of the entrepreneurial flair their heirs and successors
20 would bring to so many trade sectors in the city.

The early Italians found the route to Glaswegian hearts through their stomachs as they set up chains of chip shops and ice-cream parlours; the
25 Chinese, too, helped the local palate become rather more discerning when they began to arrive in numbers half a century ago.

All of these immigrant populations have two things in common: they were economic migrants and their effect on their adopted homeland has
30 been, almost without exception, a beneficial one. That is a lesson from history some of our more hysteria-prone politicians would do well to ponder as they devise ever more unfriendly welcomes for those who would come here today to live and work.

35 This week the Home Secretary was assuring his French counterpart that Britain would clamp down even more severely on those working here illegally. At the same time plans are advanced for "accommodation centres", which will have the
40 immediate effect of preventing natural integration, while children of immigrants are to be denied the harmonising effect of inter-racial schooling. Meanwhile, ever more sophisticated technology is to be employed to stem the numbers
45 of young men who risk their lives clinging to the underside of trains and lorries, or are paying obscene sums of money to the 21st century's own version of slave traders—those traffickers in human misery who make their fortunes on the
50 back of others' desperation.

Yet at the heart of this ever more draconian approach to immigration policy lie a number of misconceptions. The UK is not a group of nations swamped by a tidal wave of immigration.
55 Relatively speaking, Europe contends with a trickle of refugees compared with countries who border areas of famine, desperate poverty, or violent political upheaval. The countries of origin of the highest numbers coming here change from
60 year to year, depending on the hotspots of global conflict. A significant proportion of refugees want nothing more than to be able to return to that homeland when conditions allow.

But, whether they are transient or would-be
65 settlers, they face an uphill battle trying to find legal employment. People with real skills and talents to offer us find themselves in the black economy, or unemployed, because of a sluggish system of processing applications, allied to
70 regulations which preclude the legal marketplace.

Surely the most sensible way to "crack down" on illegal workers is to permit legal alternatives. Not just because of woolly liberalism—though that's a perfectly decent instinct—but because of
75 enlightened self-interest. Recently, I was reading an analysis of what was happening to the economy in the Highlands and Islands. The writer welcomes the fact that the population of that area has gone up 20% in one generation. But he goes
80 on to say that "labour shortages of every kind are becoming the biggest single constraint in the way of additional economic expansion." He adds: "In principle the solution to this problem is readily available in the shape of the so-called asylum
85 seekers or economic migrants that our country, like most countries, seems determined to turn away."

While, for the most part, immigrants to the Highlands and Islands have recently come from England, the future lies in casting the net much
90 wider. That would be, after all, yet another Scottish solution to a Scottish problem, given that this nation regularly suffers from population loss, exporting tranches of economic migrants all over the world every year. It's been something of a
95 national hobby, which is why there is almost no corner of the globe where you won't stumble over a Caledonian society enthusiastically peopled by folks who will do anything for the old country bar
100 live in it.

Yet Ireland has managed to attract its young entrepreneurs back to help drive a burgeoning economy. We must try to do likewise. We need

immigrants. We cannot grow the necessary skills
105 fast enough to fill the gap sites. We need people
with energy and commitment and motivation,
three characteristics commonly found among those
whose circumstances prompt them to make huge
sacrifices to find a new life.

110 Round about now, families all over Scotland will be
waving their newly graduated offspring off on the
increasingly popular gap year between university
and real life. Most of them will have a ball, finding
enough work to keep the adventure on the road as
they travel. Some of them won't come back at all, 115
having found a good job or a soulmate elsewhere.
Provided they stay on the right side of the law, very
few of them will be harassed by customs officials,
locked up in detention centres while their papers
are checked, or deported for overstaying their 120
welcome. If you're one of us and sort of solvent,
come into the parlour, there's a welcome there for
you.

PASSAGE 2

The second passage is adapted from an essay in The Guardian *newspaper, also in June 2002. In it, Anne Karpf explores past and present press coverage of immigration issues and tells the story of one family from Kosovo who sought asylum in Britain.*

WE HAVE BEEN HERE BEFORE

There's a melancholy little game that staff at the
Refugee Council sometimes play. They show
visitors press cuttings about refugees and asylum
seekers from the 1900s, 1930s and today, and ask
5 them to guess when they were published. Most
people get it wrong. They assume that Jewish
refugees were welcomed, at least in the 1930s, with
a tolerance that has traditionally been seen as a
beacon of Britishness. They're shocked to discover
10 that rabid intolerance has a strong British pedigree.

And the press has persisted in peddling incorrect
figures about immigration. One newspaper's
assertion in 1938 that there were more Jews in
Britain than Germany ever had, was plain wrong.
15 Similarly, the tabloids' current depiction of Britain
as an international magnet for asylum seekers is
totally misleading. Most of the world's refugees do
what they've always done: they move from one poor
country to another, usually a neighbouring one.
20 Only a tiny percentage make it to the richer
countries: 5% to Europe, and less than 1% to
Britain. A regular peruser of the press today,
however, with its loose talk of "swamping" and
"floods", would be stunned to learn that, of 15 EU
25 countries, Britain stands at number 10 in the
number of asylum seekers per head of population.

The asylum seeker has become a composite, almost
mythical figure. Despite the allegedly vast
numbers of them now in the country, most British
30 people have never actually met one, making it all
the easier to dehumanise them.

But what does real asylum-seeking feel like?
Thirty-one-year-old Arberore arrived with her
husband, Petrit, and their two-year-old son Norik
35 from Pristina, Kosovo, in 1995 as illegal asylum
seekers. Petrit, a travel agent, had been questioned
and threatened on many occasions by Serb police,
while Arberore, an architecture student, could no
longer attend the university because it was closed to
40 Albanians. "We felt that we were in danger," she
says, "but it was a very difficult decision to leave
because we were a very close-knit community."

They arrived in Britain on false papers. "It was
very scary—it was the first time in my life that I lied
like that. I felt terrible. Petrit's hand was shaking 45
when he handed over the papers." Upon arrival,
they went straight to the Home Office, to tell them
that they'd entered with false papers. "They didn't
threaten to deport us, because we had a child," says
Arberore, "but we were scared. We spent the day 50
waiting in the Home Office. I felt so happy that I
wasn't any longer in Kosovo to be frightened, but I
felt like a beggar that day. We had to be
fingerprinted. I thought I was going to prison." It
took them two years to get legal asylum.   55

I showed Arberore, now a student at Middlesex
University, some press cuttings on asylum seekers.
She was particularly shocked by one headline
A DOOR WE CAN'T CLOSE. She said, "It
makes me feel like vermin." And of another GET 60
THEM OUT, she demanded, "Who wrote that? It
makes me feel as if I'm no one. I can give something
to this country. But I want to say to these reporters:
we're all human beings and who knows when
British people might need someone's help? We left 65
everything there: we had a job, a huge house and a
garden; we had a nice life. But the most important
thing was our freedom."

Rabbi Hugo Gryn once said: "How you are with
someone to whom you owe nothing is a grave test." 70
At the moment, Britain is failing that test,
especially in its press coverage. The reporting of
prewar Jewish asylum seekers is shocking because
we know how that story ended. But instead of using
hindsight to idealise, we can use it to illuminate. 75
Let us learn this much at least: hostile reporting of
asylum seekers dispossesses them yet again.
Refugees seek asylum from hate or destitution, and
then run into it once more. As the daughter of
postwar Polish Jewish asylum seekers, I'm 80
stupefied by how the collective memory can be so
short, bigotry so blatant, and how, with all the
recent interest in the Holocaust, basic connections
can fail to be made. Are we doomed always to
stigmatise the stranger? Must compassion only 85
ever be extended after the event?

Questions on Passage 1

Marks | Code

1. Look at the first paragraph (lines 1–10).

   (a) By referring closely to these lines, show how you are helped to understand the meaning of the expression "diverse cultural heritage" (line 7). **2 U**

   (b) Referring to **one** example of effective word choice in this paragraph, show how the writer makes clear her positive attitude to the people she is describing. **2 A**

2. Comment on the impact of line 11 in helping the writer to develop her line of thought. **2 A**

3. From lines 12–26, identify briefly and in your own words as far as possible:

   (a) **two** similarities between Jewish and Asian immigrants to Glasgow; **2 U**

   (b) **one** similarity between Italian and Chinese immigrants to Glasgow. **1 U**

4. Read lines 27–50.

   (a) Explain in your own words the "two things" which, according to the writer, "all of these immigrant populations . . . have in common" (lines 27–28). **2 U**

   (b) Show how the writer's word choice in the sentence "That is . . . and work" (lines 31–34) makes clear her attitude to certain politicians. Refer to **two** examples in your answer. **2 A**

   (c) How does the writer's language make clear her disapproval of any **one** of the proposed measures referred to in lines 35–50? **2 A**

5. (a) Referring to specific words or phrases, show how the sentence "Yet . . . misconceptions" (lines 51–53) performs a linking function in the writer's line of thought. **2 U**

   (b) Discuss how effective you find the writer's use of imagery in lines 51–70 in making her point clear. You may refer in your answer to one or more examples. **2 E**

6. Read carefully lines 71–100.

   Using your own words as far as possible, outline **three** important points which are made in these paragraphs to develop the argument about immigration. **3 U**

7. Show how the writer uses sentence structure **or** tone to demonstrate her strength of feeling in lines 101–109. **2 A**

8. The writer concludes with a reference to Scottish students and the "gap year". How effective do you find this illustration as a conclusion to the passage as a whole? **2 E**

(26)

Questions on Passage 2

9. Look at the opening paragraph (lines 1–10).

   (a) What is the purpose of the "little game that staff at the Refugee Council sometimes play"? **1 U**

   (b) Select **one** example of imagery from these lines and explain how the writer uses it to make her point clear. **2 A**

10. Look at lines 11–26.

    (a) Using your own words as far as possible, explain briefly how the writer illustrates the idea that "the press has persisted in peddling incorrect figures about immigration" (lines 11–12). **2 U**

    (b) Show how the writer's language in lines 11–26 demonstrates her disapproval of the press. **2 A**

11. " . . . a composite, almost mythical figure" (lines 27–28).

    (a) Explain this expression in your own words. **2 U**

    (b) Explain why, according to lines 27–31, the asylum seeker is now regarded in this way. **1 U**

12. (a) In lines 32–55, the writer tells the story of a "real asylum-seeking" family.

    Discuss how successful you think the writer has been in convincing you that this is a "real" story. In your answer you should refer closely to specific features of the writing. **4 A/E**

    (b) By referring to tone **or** to sentence structure in lines 56–68, show how you are made aware of how strongly Arberore feels about the press cuttings. **2 A**

13. Show how the final paragraph (lines 69–86) brings the passage to an emotional conclusion. **3 A**

(19)

Question on both Passages

14. Which passage has given you a clearer understanding of key issues concerning immigration and asylum-seeking? You should refer in your answer to the main ideas of both passages. **5 U/E**

[END OF QUESTION PAPER] **Total (50)**

X115/302

NATIONAL QUALIFICATIONS 2003	FRIDAY, 16 MAY 10.50 AM – 12.20 PM	ENGLISH HIGHER Critical Essay

Answer **two** questions.

Each question must be taken from a different section.

Each question is worth 25 marks.

SCOTTISH QUALIFICATIONS AUTHORITY

©

Answer TWO questions from this paper.

Each question must be chosen from a different Section (A–E). You are not allowed to choose two questions from the same Section.

In all Sections you may use Scottish texts.

Write the number of each question chosen in the margin of your answer booklet and begin each essay on a fresh page. You should spend about 45 minutes on each essay.

The following will be assessed:

- **the relevance of your essays to the questions you have chosen**

- **the quality of your answers**

- **the technical accuracy of your writing.**

Each answer is worth up to 25 marks. The total for this paper is 50 marks.

SECTION A—DRAMA

1. Choose a play in which a character feels increasingly isolated from the community in which he or she lives.

    Show how the dramatist makes you aware of the character's increasing isolation and discuss how it affects your attitude to the character.

    In your answer you must refer closely to the text and to at least **two** of: characterisation, soliloquy, key scene(s), setting, or any other appropriate feature.

2. Choose a play in which the dramatist explores conflict between opposing values or ideas.

    Show how the dramatist makes you aware of the conflict and discuss the extent to which you find the resolution of the conflict satisfying.

    In your answer you must refer closely to the text and to at least **two** of: structure, theme, key scene(s), characterisation, or any other appropriate feature.

3. Choose a play in which there is a scene which provides a clear turning point in the drama.

    Explain why it is a turning point and go on to discuss the importance of the scene to your appreciation of the play as a whole.

    In your answer you must refer closely to the text and to at least **two** of: structure, theme, dialogue, conflict, or any other appropriate feature.

4. Choose a play in which there is a breakdown in family relationship(s).

    Explain the reason(s) for the breakdown and discuss the extent to which it is important to the play as a whole.

    In your answer you must refer closely to the text and to at least **two** of: theme, dialogue, characterisation, conflict, or any other appropriate feature.

SECTION B—PROSE

5. Choose a **novel** which caused you to reconsider your views on an important human issue.

    Explain what the issue is and go on to discuss how the writer made you reconsider your views.

    In your answer you must refer closely to the text and to at least **two** of: theme, narrative stance, characterisation, climax, or any other appropriate feature.

6. Choose a **novel** or **short story** in which a conflict between two of the main characters is central to the story.

    Explain how the conflict arises and go on to discuss in detail how the writer uses it to explore an important theme.

    In your answer you must refer closely to the text and to at least **two** of: characterisation, key incident(s), structure, setting, or any other appropriate feature.

7. Choose a **novel** which you enjoyed because of the effectiveness of its ending.

    Explain how the ending satisfies you and adds to your appreciation of the novel.

    In your answer you must refer closely to the text and to at least **two** of: climax, theme, characterisation, plot, or any other appropriate feature.

8. Choose a **novel** or **short story** in which a technique (such as symbolism) is used by the author and is, in your view, vital to the success of the text.

    Explain how the writer employs this technique and why, in your opinion, it is so important to your appreciation of the text.

    In your answer you must refer closely to the text and to its theme as well as to the writer's use of your chosen technique.

9. Choose a **non-fiction text** which influenced your views about a scientific or a health-related issue.

    Outline the nature of the issue and explain how the writer's presentation influenced your views.

    In your answer you must refer closely to the text and to at least **two** of: ideas, use of evidence, structure, stance, or any other appropriate feature.

10. Choose a **non-fiction text** which tells the life story of someone who captured your interest.

    Give a brief account of what was notable about the person's achievements. Go on to discuss how the writer's presentation confirmed or changed your opinion of the individual's life.

    In your answer you must refer closely to the text and to at least **two** of: selection of information, language, narrative voice, anecdote, or any other appropriate feature.

11. Choose a **non-fiction text** which is set in a society which is different from your own.

    Explain what is significantly different and discuss how effectively the writer made you aware of this.

    In your answer you must refer closely to the text and to at least **two** of: ideas, setting in time or place, narrative voice, language, or any other appropriate feature.

[Turn over

SECTION C—POETRY

12. Choose two nature poems.

    Compare each poem's treatment of the subject, and discuss which you find more successful.

    In your answer you must refer closely to the text and to at least **two** of: atmosphere, structure, theme, imagery, or any other appropriate feature.

13. Choose a poem in which you feel there is a significant moment which reveals the central idea of the poem.

    Show how the poet achieves this in an effective way.

    In your answer you must refer closely to the text and to at least **two** of: structure, mood, imagery, ideas, or any other appropriate feature.

14. Choose a poem in which the poet has created a perfect blend of form and content.

    Show how the poet achieves this and discuss how it adds to your appreciation of the poem.

    In your answer you must refer closely to the text and to at least **two** of: form, theme, word choice, rhythm, or any other appropriate feature.

15. Choose a poem which explores **either** the significance of the past **or** the importance of family relationships.

    Show how the poet treats the subject, and explain to what extent you find the treatment convincing.

    In your answer you must refer closely to the text and to at least **two** of: theme, imagery, rhyme, tone, or any other appropriate feature.

SECTION D—MASS MEDIA

16. Choose a film in which one of the characters is corrupted by the society which surrounds him/her.

    Briefly describe how the corruption takes hold, and go on to show how the film maker involves you in the fate of the character.

    In your answer you must refer closely to the text and to at least **two** of: characterisation, mise-en-scène, theme, editing, or any other appropriate feature.

17. Choose a film in which there is a sequence creating a high degree of tension.

    Show what techniques are employed to create and sustain the tension in this sequence and how, in the context of the whole film, it adds to your viewing experience.

    In your answer you must refer closely to the text and to at least **two** of: editing, use of camera, soundtrack, mise-en-scène, or any other appropriate feature.

18. Choose a film or *TV drama which deals with a topical issue in a memorable way.

    Explain briefly what the issue is, and go on to discuss how your interest and emotions were engaged by the treatment of the issue in the film or *TV drama.

    In your answer you must refer closely to the text and to at least **two** of: theme, characterisation, mise-en-scène, structure, or any other appropriate feature.

19. Choose a film or *TV drama which makes a major part of its impact through the detailed recreation of a period setting.

    Discuss to what extent the setting contributed to your understanding of the concerns of the society depicted in the film or *TV drama.

    In your answer you must refer closely to the text and to at least **two** of: mise-en-scène, theme, music, editing, or any other appropriate feature.

*"TV drama" includes a single play, a series or a serial.

SECTION E—LANGUAGE

20. Consider an aspect of language which shows development over time.

Describe the changes which you have identified, and evaluate the gains and losses to the language.

You must refer to specific examples, and to at least **two** of the following: vocabulary, register, grammar, idiom, or any other appropriate concept.

21. Consider some aspects of language which you have identified within a particular vocational group.

Identify some of the characteristics of the language within such a group and evaluate the advantages and disadvantages for the group and the wider public.

You must refer to specific examples and to at least **two** of the following: jargon, register, technical terminology, abbreviations, or any other appropriate concept.

22. Consider the language associated with any one form of electronic communication.

Show how this language has developed and discuss to what extent it has made communication more effective.

You must refer to specific examples and to at least **two** of the following: register, technical terminology, word choice, tone, or any other appropriate concept.

23. Consider your personal use of language in different contexts.

Describe your use of language in at least two contexts, and discuss to what extent your communication varies in effectiveness from context to context.

You must refer to specific examples and to at least **two** of the following: register, dialect, accent, vocabulary, or any other appropriate concept.

[END OF QUESTION PAPER]

[BLANK PAGE]

[BLANK PAGE]

X115/301

NATIONAL　　　　　　　FRIDAY, 14 MAY　　　　　ENGLISH
QUALIFICATIONS　　　 9.00 AM – 10.30 AM　　　HIGHER
2004　　　　　　　　　　　　　　　　　　　　　　　　Close Reading

Answer all questions.

50 marks are allocated to this paper.

There are TWO passages and questions in this paper.

Read the passages carefully and then answer all the questions which follow. **Use your own words whenever possible and particularly when you are instructed to do so.**

You should read the passages to:

understand what the writers are saying about the ideas in a book by Frank Furedi called *Paranoid Parenting* (**Understanding—U**);

analyse their choices of language, imagery and structures to recognise how they convey their points of view and contribute to the impact of the passage (**Analysis—A**);

evaluate how effectively they have achieved their purpose (**Evaluation—E**).

A code letter (U, A, E) is used alongside each question to give some indication of the skills being assessed. The number of marks attached to each question will give some indication of the length of answer required.

SCOTTISH
QUALIFICATIONS
AUTHORITY

©

PASSAGE 1

The first passage is adapted from an article in The Herald *newspaper in February 2002. In it, Melanie Reid strongly supports the ideas in a book called* Paranoid Parenting *by Frank Furedi.*

IS PARANOID PARENTING THE GREATEST DANGER TO OUR KIDS?

If you read a wonderful new book by sociologist Frank Furedi—*Paranoid Parenting*—you will see the story of a teacher who quit the profession after a school trip was cancelled. Some parents
5 were worried the trip would involve their children in a 45-minute journey in a private car. Would the cars be roadworthy? Were the drivers experienced? Were these no-smoking cars?

Here's another story: once upon a time, there was
10 a little boy who got a new pair of wellies, inside which, around the top, his mother inscribed his name in felt pen. This child, asserting the inalienable rights of small boys everywhere, then proceeded to go out and fill his wellies with water.
15 The ink of his name ran, and by the time the bell rang for school that Monday morning the small boy had vivid blue smudges, like vicious bruises, ringing his calves. His teacher, a zealous young woman, ever alert to the omnipresence of evil,
20 took one look at the marks and lifted the phone to the social work department. "Come quickly," she hissed. "This boy is clearly being abused."

When the social workers rushed to examine the boy and quiz his mother, they could find evidence
25 of nothing. Soap and water had washed away the dreadful bruises, and the mother's relationship with her son turned out to be impeccably healthy. The only mistake this unfortunate family had made was to fulfil society's constant, lurking
30 expectation that all children are in danger all the time.

This may be an urban myth. It matters not. A fairy tale's power lies in its ability to express authentic fears—and this one reveals the
35 paranoia that now prevails where bringing up children is concerned.

We live in an age where parental paranoia has reached absurd heights. Collectively we are now convinced that our children's survival is
40 permanently under threat; worse still, we believe that every incident concerning a child, however benign or accidental, is immediately regarded as a case of bad parenting. We live under perpetual suspicion; and in turn we project it on to everyone
45 around us.

Inevitably, this paranoia has fuelled an artful kind of job creation. When something terrible happens—a sledging accident, a fall from a tree, a scare about "dangerous" foods—the sirens sound
50 and the blue lights flash. This is not just the arrival of the ambulance: it is also a metaphor for the extensive child protection industry gearing

itself up for another bout of self-importance. Mee-maw, mee-maw. Clear the area, please. This is a job for the expert doom-mongers. 55

I am tired of these prophets of death and injury. I do not need the Royal Society for the Prevention of Accidents to tell me that children should wear helmets while sledging, because I am incensed at the thought of the hundreds of kids whose 60 parents will now ban them from sledging on the five-million-to-one chance that they might hit a tree. I mourn also for the kids who will never know the delight of cycling with the wind in their hair, or climbing up trees, or exploring hidden 65 places. Growing up devoid of freedom, decision-making, and the opportunity to learn from taking their own risks, our children are becoming trapped, neurotic, and as genetically weakened as battery hens. 70

I am fed up listening to scaremongers about the E-coli virus, telling me my child should never visit a farm or come into contact with animals. I am weary of organisations that are dedicated to promulgating the idea that threats and dangers to 75 children lurk everywhere. I am sick of charities who on the one hand attack overprotective parents and at the same time say children should never be left unsupervised in public places.

Everywhere you turn there is an army of 80 professionals—ably abetted by the media—hard at work encouraging parents to fear the worst. Don't let your children out in the sun—not unless they're wearing special UV-resistant T-shirts. Don't buy your children a Wendy house, they 85 might crush their fingers in the hinges. Don't buy a baby walker, your toddlers might brain themselves. Don't buy plastic baby teethers, your baby might suck in harmful chemicals. Don't let them use mobile phones, they'll sizzle 90 their brains. Don't buy a second-hand car seat, it will not protect them. And on and on it goes.

Teachers are giving up teaching, and youth organisations are dying because they can't find adults prepared to run them. Everywhere good, 95 inspirational people are turning their backs on children because they are terrified of the children and their parents turning on them, accusing them of all manner of wrongdoing. They can no longer operate, they say, in a climate of suspicion and fear. 100

I know how they feel. Some years ago I organised an event for my child's primary school—a running and cycling race along popular, well-used Forestry Commission cycle-tracks.

105 For safety, parents were to be paired with their offspring; we laid on enough insurance and first aid for a B-list royal wedding. Yet the event was almost called off the night before when I received worried calls from parents who had

110 been out to inspect the route. The track was far too rough, they said. The risk of children injuring themselves was too great. It was too dangerous to proceed. As it happened, we did go ahead and everyone had a wonderful time.

115 Children glowed with achievement and self-esteem, unaware of the crisis of parental nerve which overshadowed the whole day.

But so deep are we in the pit of exaggerated, irrational risk-perception that we have moved from the awareness that things might go wrong 120 to the assumption that things *will* go wrong. It is a dangerous spiral. For our children, who in reality are overwhelmingly safer than they have ever been in history from death, disease, accident, or injury, it is more than dangerous. It 125 is utterly catastrophic.

PASSAGE 2

The second passage is from an article in The Guardian *newspaper, in June 2002. In it, Catherine Bennett takes a slightly less enthusiastic view of Furedi's ideas.*

PROTECTIVE PARENTS, YES. BUT PARANOID?

It seems the childcare pendulum has swung: the principal threat to children is no longer neglectful parents, but excessively protective ones who are always worrying about germs.

5 Frank Furedi, reader in sociology at the University of Kent, has written a book, *Paranoid Parenting*, in which he explores the causes and far-reaching consequences of too much cosseting. "It is always important to recall that

10 our obsession with our children's safety is likely to be more damaging to them than any risks that they are likely to meet with in their daily encounter with the world," Furedi writes.

So, far from fretting, like paranoid parents,

15 about the risks of physical injury, Furedi seems almost nostalgic about them: "Playground areas are now covered with rubber to limit the damage when a child does fall." Should they, perhaps, be constructed from something more challenging:

20 shards of broken glass, say, or the traditional grit which was once so successful at lacerating young knees, insinuating itself so deeply into the exposed tissue that it could only be removed by a pair of bacteria-infested tweezers?

25 Elsewhere, exploring the degree to which children's lives are now circumscribed by parental cowardy custards, Furedi mentions the dramatic reduction in the number of children walking to school. In Britain, he notes, parents

30 are more likely to drive their children to school "than in Germany, Scandinavia or America, where the distance between home and school

may be far greater". Alas for Furedi's campaign, some figures published this week are likely to encourage yet more of this protective behaviour 35 and may even help promote parental paranoia. A report from UNICEF has found that children in Britain are among the safest in the world: safer, for instance, than in Germany, and far safer than those in America. British children are safer, it 40 seems, precisely because so many of them are now driven to and from school.

People like Furedi seem to hanker for the time when bright-eyed schoolboys would think nothing of trudging several hundred miles to 45 school in their threadbare socks, negotiating such major arterial roads as existed in the olden days, sustained only by a few strands of linty liquorice and the prospect of a tepid miniature of school milk. Such hazards as the young scamps 50 might meet along the way—electrical storms, say, or runaway trains, or a modest invasion of Martians—merely added to the character-building nature of the exercise.

Perhaps parents who would, given a choice, 55 prefer their children to be minimally hurt when they fall off a climbing frame or into a pond are not being paranoid—just being careful. Maybe the real paranoiacs are not those who worry about their children being squashed by 60 sociopaths in cars, but those who insist on adding the consequences of mollycoddling to the already overlong catalogue of parental anxieties.

Questions on Passage 1

		Marks	Code

1. How does the story told in the first paragraph (lines 1–8) help you to understand the meaning of the word "paranoid"? — **2** — **U**

2. Read the story the writer tells in lines 9–31.

   (a) State briefly the main point of this story in conveying the writer's argument. — **1** — **U**

   (b) How does the writer's word choice in these lines make clear her attitude **either** to the teacher **or** to the social workers? — **2** — **A**

3. "It matters not." (line 32)

   Explain in your own words why the writer believes it is not important whether this story is true or not. — **2** — **U**

4. Read lines 37–55.

   (a) How does the writer's language in lines 37–45 emphasise her belief that "parental paranoia has reached absurd heights" (lines 37–38)? — **2** — **A**

   (b) (i) What is the writer's attitude to "the expert doom-mongers" (line 55)? — **1** — **U**

   (ii) How does her language in lines 46–55 make this attitude clear? — **2** — **A**

5. "...as genetically weakened as battery hens..." (lines 69–70)

   (a) Why, according to the writer, are modern children in danger of becoming like this? Refer to lines 56–70 and use your own words as far as possible in your answer. — **2** — **U**

   (b) How effective do you find the image of "battery hens" in conveying the writer's view of the way children are currently being brought up? — **2** — **A/E**

6. Read lines 71–92.

   (a) (i) Identify the tone of lines 71–79. — **1** — **A**

   (ii) Explain how this tone is conveyed. — **2** — **A**

   (b) How does the language of lines 80–92 emphasise the writer's feelings about the "army of professionals" (lines 80–81)?

   In your answer you should refer to at least **two** techniques such as sentence structure, tone, word choice... — **4** — **A**

7. Why, according to the writer in lines 93–100, are teachers and youth workers "turning their backs on children" (lines 96–97)? Use your own words as far as possible in your answer. — **2** — **U**

8. How effective do you find the personal anecdote in lines 101–117 in supporting the writer's point of view in the passage so far? — **3** — **U/E**

9. By referring to **one** technique, show how the writer demonstrates in the final paragraph (lines 118–126) the intensity of her feelings on the subject. — **2** — **A**

(30)

Questions on Passage 2

10. Read lines 1–24.

    (a) Explain how the image in the opening paragraph (lines 1–4) supports the writer's point. — **2** — **A**

    (b) How does the context in which it is used help you to understand the meaning of the word "cosseting" (line 9)? — **2** — **U**

    (c) (i) Explain in your own words what Furedi thinks about modern play areas. — **1** — **U**

    (ii) What is the writer's attitude to Furedi's point of view and how is this made clear by the tone of lines 18 ("Should they...")–24? — **2** — **A**

11. "Alas for Furedi's campaign..." (line 33)

    Explain in your own words how the UNICEF report contradicts Furedi's point of view. — **2** — **U**

12. Show how the writer's attitude to Furedi's views is conveyed in lines 43–54. — **4** — **A**

13. Explain in your own words the main points the writer makes in her concluding paragraph (lines 55–64). — **2** — **U**

(15)

Question on both Passages

14. Which writer's response to Furedi's views are you more inclined to agree with?

    You must refer closely to the ideas of both passages as evidence for your answer. — **5** — **U/E**

(5)

[END OF QUESTION PAPER]

Total (50)

X115/302

NATIONAL
QUALIFICATIONS
2004

FRIDAY, 14 MAY
10.50 AM – 12.20 PM

ENGLISH
HIGHER
Critical Essay

[Open out for Questions]

Answer **two** questions.

Each question must be taken from a different section.

Each question is worth 25 marks.

SCOTTISH
QUALIFICATIONS
AUTHORITY

©

Answer TWO questions from this paper.

Each question must be chosen from a different Section (A–E). You are not allowed to choose two questions from the same Section.

In all Sections you may use Scottish texts.

Write the number of each question chosen in the margin of your answer booklet and begin each essay on a fresh page. You should spend about 45 minutes on each essay.

The following will be assessed:

- **the relevance of your essays to the questions you have chosen**

- **the quality of your writing**

- **the technical accuracy of your writing.**

Each answer is worth up to 25 marks. The total for this paper is 50 marks.

SECTION A—DRAMA

1. Choose a play in which your attitude to a central character varies at different stages of the action.

    Show how the skill of the dramatist causes your attitude to change.

    In your answer you must refer closely to the text and to at least **two** of: characterisation, language, key scene(s), setting, or any other appropriate feature.

2. Choose a play in which the dramatist explores the idea of rebellion against authority.

    Explain briefly the circumstances which give rise to the rebellion and discuss how successfully you think the dramatist explores the idea.

    In your answer you must refer closely to the text and to at least **two** of: theme, soliloquy, conflict, characterisation, or any other appropriate feature.

3. Choose a play in which there is a scene involving intense emotion.

    Show how the dramatist makes you aware of the intensity of the emotion in the scene and discuss the importance of the scene to the drama as a whole.

    In your answer you must refer closely to the text and to at least **two** of: conflict, characterisation, soliloquy, dialogue, or any other appropriate feature.

4. Choose a play which you have read and watched in performance.

    Compare your reading of a key scene with its presentation in performance.

    In your answer you must refer closely to the text and to at least **two** of: dialogue, characterisation, casting, stage set, or any other appropriate feature.

SECTION B—PROSE

5. Choose a **novel** in which your admiration for a particular character grows as the plot unfolds.

   Explain briefly why your admiration increases and, in more detail, discuss how the writer achieves this.

   In your answer you must refer closely to the text and to at least **two** of: characterisation, theme, key incidents, structure, or any other appropriate feature.

6. Choose a **novel** or **short story** in which the writer's use of setting in time and/or place has a significant part to play in your appreciation of the text as a whole.

   Give the relevant details of the setting and then discuss fully why it has such significance.

   In your answer you must refer closely to the text and to at least **two** of: setting, narrative stance, theme, characterisation, or any other appropriate feature.

7. Choose a **novel** which had such an impact on you that you still reflect upon its message.

   Explain why the novel has had such an impact on you.

   In your answer you must refer closely to the text and to at least **two** of: theme, key incidents, characterisation, structure, or any other appropriate feature.

8. Choose a **novel** or **short story** which reaches a climax which you find dramatic or moving or disturbing.

   Explain how the writer achieves the effect and discuss how it contributes to your appreciation of the text as a whole.

   In your answer you must refer closely to the text and to at least **two** of: structure, theme, characterisation, dialogue, or any other appropriate feature.

9. Choose a **non-fiction text** in which the writer puts forward an opinion which you found totally convincing.

   Explain what the writer's view is and, in more detail, discuss how this view was presented in a way that convinced you.

   In your answer you must refer closely to the text and to at least **two** of: ideas, evidence, stance, style, or any other appropriate feature.

10. Choose a **non-fiction text** which increased your interest in a particular leisure activity.

    Give a brief description of the activity and explain, in more detail, what it was about the writer's presentation of it that captured your interest.

    In your answer you must refer closely to the text and to at least **two** of: choice of detail, anecdote, language, structure, or any other appropriate feature.

11. Choose a **non-fiction text** in which the writer's ability to evoke a sense of place is very important to the success of the text.

    Show how the writer's presentation of the location(s) enhanced your appreciation of the text.

    In your answer you must refer closely to the text and to at least **two** of: setting, anecdote, stance, mood, or any other appropriate feature.

[Turn over

SECTION C—POETRY

12. Choose a poem in which the poet explores the significance of the passage of time.

    Explain why the passage of time is significant in this poem and discuss the means by which the poet explores its significance.

    In your answer you must refer closely to the text and to at least **two** of: mood, form, theme, imagery, or any other appropriate feature.

13. Choose **two** love poems.

    By comparing the treatment of the subject in each poem, discuss which you find more successful.

    In your answer you must refer closely to the text and to at least **two** of: structure, word choice, imagery, sound, or any other appropriate feature.

14. Choose a poem in which a chance encounter or a seemingly unimportant incident acquires increased significance by the end of the poem.

    Show how the poet's development of the encounter or incident leads you to a deeper understanding of the poem's theme.

    In your answer you must refer closely to the text and to at least **two** of: theme, atmosphere, word choice, rhythm, or any other appropriate feature.

15. Choose a poem in which the poet creates a picture of a heroic or a corrupt figure.

    Discuss the means by which the personality is clearly depicted.

    In your answer you must refer closely to the text and to at least **two** of: imagery, tone, rhyme, word choice, or any other appropriate feature.

SECTION D—MASS MEDIA

16. Choose a film which belongs to a specific genre such as horror, fantasy, film noir, western.

    How well did the film exploit or develop the features of the genre in dealing with its subject matter?

    In your answer you must refer closely to the text and to at least **two** of: mise-en-scène, soundtrack, editing, casting, or any other appropriate feature.

17. Choose a *TV drama in which conflict between or within groups, factions or families provides a major interest.

    Describe the nature of the conflict and show how this conflict is presented to sustain your interest in the drama.

    In your answer you must refer closely to the text and to at least **two** of: structure, characterisation, setting, use of camera, or any other appropriate feature.

18. Choose a film which casts light on an issue of political, social or moral concern.

    Identify the issue and show how the film makers illuminated it for you.

    In your answer you must refer closely to the text and to at least **two** of: theme, mise-en-scène, editing, plot, or any other appropriate feature.

19. Choose an important character from a film or *TV drama whose presentation in your opinion has outstanding visual impact.

    Briefly outline the importance of this character in the film or drama and go on to show how the character is developed primarily through images.

    In your answer you must refer closely to the text and to at least **two** of: mise-en-scène, characterisation, editing, casting, or any other appropriate feature.

*"TV drama" can be a single play, a series or a serial.

SECTION E—LANGUAGE

20. Consider the language of persuasion as used in the political or commercial world.

    By referring to one such persuasive use of language, discuss how successful you feel it was in fulfilling its purpose.

    You must refer to specific examples and to at least **two** of the following: word choice, tone, presentation, structure, or any other appropriate feature.

21. Consider the spoken language of a particular locality.

    Identify some of the characteristics of the language of this locality and discuss to what extent it fulfils a valuable function within the community.

    You must refer to specific examples and to at least **two** of the following: dialect, accent, vocabulary, register, or any other appropriate feature.

22. Consider the language of newspaper reporting (broadsheet and/or tabloid) associated with such subjects as war, sport, crime, environmental disasters.

    Identify some of the characteristics of this language and discuss how effective you feel it was in conveying the events described.

    You must refer to specific examples and to at least **two** of the following: word choice, illustration, presentation, point of view, or any other appropriate feature.

23. Consider the language associated with a particular group in society which shares a common interest or background.

    Identify the aspects of language which are special to this group and discuss to what extent these aspects facilitate communication within the group.

    You must refer to specific examples and to at least **two** of the following: word choice, register, abbreviation, jargon, or any other appropriate feature.

[END OF QUESTION PAPER]

[BLANK PAGE]

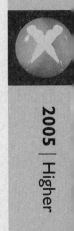

[BLANK PAGE]

X115/301

NATIONAL
QUALIFICATIONS
2005

FRIDAY, 13 MAY
9.00 AM – 10.30 AM

ENGLISH
HIGHER
Close Reading

Answer all questions.

50 marks are allocated to this paper.

There are TWO passages and questions.

Read the passages carefully and then answer all the questions which follow. **Use your own words whenever possible and particularly when you are instructed to do so.**

You should read the passages to:

understand what the writers are saying about the threat to earth from comets and asteroids (**Understanding—U**);

analyse their choices of language, imagery and structures to recognise how they convey their points of view and contribute to the impact of the passage (**Analysis—A**);

evaluate how effectively they have achieved their purpose (**Evaluation—E**).

A code letter (U, A, E) is used alongside each question to give some indication of the skills being assessed. The number of marks attached to each question will give some indication of the length of answer required.

THB X115/301 6/42870

SCOTTISH
QUALIFICATIONS
AUTHORITY

PASSAGE 1

The first passage is the Introduction to a book called "IMPACT! The Threat of Comets and Asteroids" by Gerrit L Verschuur, a well-known scientist. He explores past impacts caused by comets and asteroids and goes on to look at the probability of further collisions. He raises questions about the future of the human race and asks what, in light of the knowledge we have, we should do now.

THE THREAT OF COMETS AND ASTEROIDS

The discovery that a comet impact triggered the disappearance of the dinosaurs as well as more than half the species that lived 65 million years ago may have been the most significant scientific
5 breakthrough of the twentieth century. Brilliant detective work on the part of hundreds of scientists in analysing clues extracted from the study of fossils, and by counting the objects in near-earth space, has allowed the dinosaur
10 mass-extinction mystery to be solved. As a result we have gained new insight into the nature of life on earth.

A lot has been learned about the nature of cosmic collisions and this new knowledge has given a
15 remarkable twist to the story of our origins. We now recognise that comet and asteroid impacts may be the most important driving force behind evolutionary change on the planet. Originally, such objects smashed into one another to build
20 the earth 4·5 million years ago. After that, further comet impacts brought the water of our oceans and the organic molecules needed for life. Ever since then, impacts have continued to punctuate the story of evolution. On many occasions,
25 comets slammed into earth with such violence that they nearly precipitated the extinction of all life. In the aftermath of each catastrophe, new species emerged to take the place of those that had been wiped out.

30 We have now recognised the fundamental role of comet and asteroid collisions in shaping evolutionary change and this recognition means that the notion of "survival of the fittest" may have to be reconsidered. Survivors of essentially
35 random impact catastrophes—cosmic accidents —were those creatures who just happened to be "lucky" enough to find themselves alive after the dust settled. It doesn't matter how well a creature may have been able to survive in a particular
40 environment *before* the event—being thumped on the head by a large object from space *during* the event is not conducive to a long and happy existence.

Our new understanding of why the dinosaurs
45 and so many of their contemporary species became extinct has revealed the earth as a planet not specifically designed for our well-being. From time to time, life is rudely interrupted by shattering events on a scale we can barely
50 imagine.

For more than two centuries the possibility that the earth might be struck by comets has been debated and three questions have been raised from the start: will a comet again hit the earth;
55 might comet impact lead to the extinction of mankind; is it possible that the flood legends from so many world cultures could be explained by past comet impact in the oceans which triggered enormous tsunamis? In recent years
60 most scientists have come to accept that the answer to the first two questions is probably yes.

The third of these questions has begun again to excite interest, but here the implications of an affirmative answer reach beyond the scientific.
65 Great prejudice exists both for and against the idea that the legendary "Flood" was a real event triggered by asteroid or comet impact. To accept this possibility challenges the long-held beliefs of many people who see the event as having religious
70 significance. However, recent breakthroughs in our understanding of cosmic collisions have cast new light on what might lie behind ancient beliefs, legends, sagas and myths that tell of terrible floods that once ravaged the world.

75 In comparison with more immediate threats to the continued survival of our species (acid rain, destruction of stratospheric ozone, the greenhouse effect, overpopulation), the danger of comet or asteroid impacts may seem remote.
80 The problem with impact events, however, is that their consequences are so awesome that we can barely imagine what it would be like to be struck by a large object from space. And there would be limited opportunity for reflection following such
85 an event.

There is also an irony attached to the acquisition of our knowledge of the threat of comets and asteroids. We know that cosmic collisions clearly set the scene for the emergence of *Homo sapiens*,
90 our species. We have recently become conscious enough to design and manipulate instruments such as radio-telescopes which allow us to explore beyond our senses. In so doing, we have come to behold how our species fits into the
95 cosmic scheme of things and to foresee the dangers.

Once we appreciate that impact catastrophes have shaped life as we know it, and that such events will happen again in the future, how will
100 this awareness alter the way we see ourselves in the cosmic context? Will we let nature take its course and trust to luck that our species will

105 survive the next violent collision? Or will we confront the forces that may yet influence the destiny of all life on earth?

Many details referred to in our story are still controversial. Debate is particularly heated as regards the role of impacts in directing the course of human history. All of this is very
110 exciting. The whole topic is in a state of ferment, a symptom that something significant is brewing.

Ultimately we must ask ourselves whether we find the risk of future impact to be sufficiently great to merit doing something to avoid it.
115 Many dangers posed by living in a modern technological society are far more likely to cost us our lives, but that is not the point. Rare comet or asteroid impacts may cost *all* of us our lives. So how will the threat of comets and asteroids fit
120 into our thinking? We can only answer this question after we have learned a great deal more about the nature of the danger.

PASSAGE 2

The second passage is adapted from an article in a national tabloid newspaper.

ASTEROID COULD BLAST US BACK TO DARK AGES

It would destroy an area the size of Belgium in one and a half seconds and plunge the world back into the Dark Ages. The giant lump of space rock racing towards Earth today at 75,000
5 miles an hour would unleash a force 20 million times more powerful than the atom bomb dropped on Hiroshima in 1945. If it ends up crashing into us on 21st March 2014, that is.

Asteroid QQ47, two thirds of a mile wide, was
10 first spotted by astronomers in Mexico ten days ago and is hurtling towards us at twenty miles a second. A direct hit by the huge asteroid would send billions of tons of dust into the sky, blocking out the sun, causing plant life to perish
15 and livestock to starve. The effect on human life, too, would be devastating. But perhaps we needn't worry too much—because scientists say the chances of it hitting us are just 1 in 909,000.

Astrophysics expert, Dr Alan Fitzsimmons of
20 Queen's University, Belfast, who advises the UK NEO (Near-Earth Objects) Information Centre in Leicester, is optimistic that Earth will come through the latest asteroid scare unscathed: "In all probability, within the next
25 month we will know its future orbit with an accuracy which will mean we will be able to rule out any impact."

Others are, however, convinced that it is only a matter of time before we face Armageddon.
30 Liberal Democrat MP and sky-watcher, Lembit Opik, says: "I have said for years that the chance of an asteroid having an impact which could wipe out most of the human race is 100 per cent." He has raised his worries in the
35 Commons, successfully campaigned for an all-party task force to assess the potential risk and helped set up the Spaceguard UK facility to track near-earth objects. He admits: "It does

sound like a science fiction story and I may
40 sound like one of those guys who walk up and down with a sandwich-board saying the end of the world is nigh. But the end *is* nigh."

Asteroids have long been a source of fascination for scientists and range in size from tiny dust
45 particles to huge objects nearly 600 miles across. More than 100,000 asteroids have been classified since the first was spotted by Italian astronomer Guiseppe Piazzi in 1801. Some contain carbon-bearing compounds and
50 scientists think they could hold the key to creation. Giant meteors hitting the planet could have delivered chemicals which kick-started life on Earth.

But now asteroid QQ47 could end man's fragile
55 reign. Spaceguard director, Jay Tate, explains: "In the longer term the problem of being hit by an asteroid will be the amount of material that is injected into the Earth's atmosphere. Within two or three days the surface of the Earth will be
60 cold and dark. And it is the dark which will be the problem, because the plants will begin to die out. At best guess, we will probably lose about 25 per cent of the human population of the planet in the first six months or so. The rest of us
65 are basically back in the Middle Ages. We have got no power, no communications, no infrastructure. We are back to hunter-gathering."

Although there are hundreds of undiscovered
70 asteroids hurtling around, bookmakers are willing to take bets at odds of 909,000 to 1 that QQ47 will snuff out mankind. After all, as one bookmaker says happily: "If the asteroid does wipe out life on Earth, we probably won't have
75 to worry about paying out to winning customers."

Questions on Passage 1

			Marks	Code

1. (a) According to the first sentence of the passage, what important discovery has been made about comet impact? Use your own words as far as possible in your answer. — **2 U**

(b) By referring to lines 5–12 ("Brilliant . . . on earth."), describe briefly **one** method scientists used to find the evidence for this discovery. — **1 U**

2. (a) Explain, using your own words as far as possible, what is meant by "the most important driving force behind evolutionary change on the planet" (lines 17–18). — **2 U**

(b) Using your own words as far as possible, give any two examples from lines 18–29 which the writer uses to illustrate the point being made in lines 17–18. — **2 U**

(c) How does the language of lines 18–29 highlight the writer's ideas? You should refer to at least two of the following techniques: structure, word choice, imagery. — **4 A**

3. Read lines 30–43.

(a) Explain in your own words why the writer thinks that the theory of the "survival of the fittest" will have to be reconsidered. — **2 U**

(b) Explain how the writer creates a slightly humorous tone in lines 34–43. — **2 A**

4. What does "Our new understanding" (line 44) about the extinction of other species lead us to think about our own relationship with the planet? Use your own words as far as possible in your answer. — **1 U**

5. How does the writer's use of punctuation in lines 51–59 ("For more . . . tsunamis?") help you to understand what he is saying? — **2 A**

6. Referring to lines 62–74, explain in your own words one way in which the "third of these questions" leads into an area which may be described as "beyond the scientific" (line 64). — **2 U**

7. In lines 75–85, the writer deals with various threats to the survival of our species.

Show how effective the last sentence "And there would be . . . event." (lines 83–85) is as a conclusion to this paragraph. — **2 E**

8. Explain briefly in your own words what, according to the writer, is "an irony" about "our knowledge of the threat of comets and asteroids". You should refer to lines 86–96 in your answer. — **2 U**

9. (a) According to the writer in lines 97–105, what two possible courses of action are open to us with regard to future "impact catastrophes"? Use your own words as far as possible in your answer. — **2 U**

(b) Show how effective you find the writer's use of imagery in lines 106–112 in conveying the excitement of the "debate". — **2 A/E**

(c) Which course of action do you think the writer favours? Support your answer by close reference to lines 113–123. — **2 U**

(30)

Questions on Passage 2

10. Show how the writer captures your attention in the opening to the article (lines 1–18). You should refer to specific techniques and/or stylistic features in these lines. — **4 A**

11. By commenting on specific words or phrases in lines 19–27, show to what extent you would have confidence in Dr Alan Fitzsimmons. — **2 A/E**

12. Show how lines 28–42 help you to understand the meaning of the word "Armageddon" (line 29). — **2 U**

13. The style of writing in lines 43–53 differs from that in the preceding paragraphs.

Describe these two different styles and support your answer by brief reference to the text. — **2 A**

14. Show how Jay Tate's language (lines 56–68) emphasises the devastating effects of asteroid impact. In your answer you should refer to such features as sentence structure, verb tense, word choice . . . — **4 A**

15. Explain why the bookmaker is speaking "happily" (line 73). — **1 U**

(15)

Question on both Passages

16. Which passage do you find more effective in making you think about the implications for the human race of comet and asteroid impact? Justify your choice by referring to the **ideas and style** of **both passages**. — **5 E**

(5)

Total (50)

[END OF QUESTION PAPER]

X115/302

NATIONAL QUALIFICATIONS 2005	FRIDAY, 13 MAY 10.50 AM – 12.20 PM	ENGLISH HIGHER Critical Essay

Answer **two** questions.

Each question must be taken from a different section.

Each question is worth 25 marks.

SCOTTISH QUALIFICATIONS AUTHORITY

Answer TWO questions from this paper.

Each question must be chosen from a different Section (A–E). You are not allowed to choose two questions from the same Section.

In all Sections you may use Scottish texts.

Write the number of each question chosen in the margin of your answer booklet and begin each essay on a fresh page. You should spend about 45 minutes on each essay.

The following will be assessed:

- **the relevance of your essays to the questions you have chosen**

- **the quality of your writing**

- **the technical accuracy of your writing.**

Each answer is worth up to 25 marks. The total for this paper is 50 marks.

SECTION A—DRAMA

1. Choose a play in which a character is seeking the truth, avoiding the truth or hiding the truth.

    Explain to what extent the character achieves this aim and discuss how the dramatist uses the situation to reveal important aspects of the character's role in the play as a whole.

    In your answer you must refer closely to the text and to at least two of: characterisation, theme, key scene(s), conflict, or any other appropriate feature.

2. Choose a play which features **one** of the following themes: appearance versus reality; good versus evil; dreams versus reality; youth versus age.

    Show how the dramatist develops one of these themes and discuss how the exploration of this theme enhances your appreciation of the play as a whole.

    In your answer you must refer closely to the text and to at least two of: conflict, characterisation, key scene(s), structure, or any other appropriate feature.

3. Choose a play in which the dramatist creates a sense of mystery at or near the beginning of the play.

    Show how the dramatist creates the sense of mystery and then discuss to what extent the resolution of the mystery is important to the play as a whole.

    In your answer you must refer closely to the text and to at least two of: key scene(s), theme, setting, atmosphere, or any other appropriate feature.

4. Choose a play in which the mood is mainly dark or pessimistic.

    Show how the dramatist creates this mood and discuss how appropriate it is to the main idea(s) of the play.

    In your answer you must refer closely to the text and to at least two of: setting, theme, characterisation, dialogue, or any other appropriate feature.

SECTION B—PROSE

Prose Fiction

5. Choose a **novel** in which an incident reveals a flaw in a central character.

   Explain how the incident reveals this flaw and go on to discuss the importance of the flaw in your understanding of the character.

   In your answer you must refer closely to the text and to at least two of: key incident(s), theme, characterisation, structure, or any other appropriate feature.

6. Choose a **novel** or **short story** in which the writer's method of narration (such as first person narrative, diary form, journal . . .) plays a significant part.

   Explain briefly the method of narration and then discuss its importance to your appreciation of the text.

   In your answer you must refer closely to the text and to at least two of: narrative technique, tone, characterisation, structure, or any other appropriate feature.

7. Choose a **novel** in which the story's emotional twists ensure that your interest is held until the end.

   Briefly explain how these twists involve you in the story and then discuss how they lead to a deeper appreciation of the text as a whole.

   In your answer you must refer closely to the text and to at least two of: characterisation, structure, theme, key incident(s), or any other appropriate feature.

8. Choose a **novel** or **short story** in which the fate of a main character is important in conveying the writer's theme.

   Explain what you consider the theme to be and discuss how effectively the fate of the character conveys it.

   In your answer you must refer closely to the text and to at least two of: theme, plot, characterisation, setting, or any other appropriate feature.

Prose Non-fiction

9. Choose an example of **biography** or **autobiography** which gave you a detailed insight into a person's life.

   Explain how the writer's presentation made you think deeply about the person and his or her life.

   In your answer you must refer closely to the text and to at least two of: style, anecdotes, setting, ideas, or any other appropriate feature.

10. Choose a **non-fiction text** in which the writer's presentation of an experience triggers an emotional response from you.

    Give a brief description of the experience and, in more detail, explain how the writer's presentation has this effect.

    In your answer you must refer closely to the text and to at least two of: choice of detail, language, stance, structure, or any other appropriate feature.

11. Choose a **non-fiction text** in which the writer puts forward views on a social issue.

    Explain the writer's stance on the issue and then discuss in detail to what extent the writer's presentation influenced your point of view.

    In your answer you must refer closely to the text and to at least two of: language, evidence, stance, setting, or any other appropriate feature.

[Turn over

SECTION C—POETRY

12. Choose a poem in which a specific setting is strongly evoked.

    Show how the poet creates this sense of place and/or time, and then discuss the relative importance of the setting to the poem as a whole.

    In your answer you must refer closely to the text and to at least two of: setting, theme, mood, imagery, or any other appropriate feature.

13. Choose a poem which you feel is particularly relevant to a teenage audience.

    Make clear why you think the poem is so relevant to this age group and show how the poetic techniques used in the poem help to achieve this.

    In your answer you must refer closely to the text and to at least two of: theme, mood, imagery, rhythm, or any other appropriate feature.

14. Choose a poem in which humour (for example, satire, wit or irony) plays a significant part.

    Show how the poet makes the poem humorous and discuss how important the humour is to the underlying message of the poem.

    In your answer you must refer closely to the text and to at least two of: ideas, tone, rhyme, word choice, or any other appropriate feature.

15. Choose a poet whose writing displays great beauty.

    By referring to one **or** more than one poem, show how the writer creates this sense of beauty and go on to discuss whether or not the beauty of the writing is more important to you than the ideas explored in the poem(s).

    In your answer you must refer closely to the text(s) and to at least two of: imagery, sound, rhythm, word choice, theme, or any other appropriate feature.

SECTION D—MASS MEDIA

16. Choose a film or *TV drama in which an individual or group is threatened by an evil force.

    Briefly explain the situation and go on to show how successfully the film/programme makers use this situation to provoke audience response.

    You must refer to specific examples and to at least two of the following: characterisation, mise-en-scène, editing, soundtrack, or any other appropriate feature.

17. Choose a film or *TV drama in which a particular mood is constructed through key images and elements of the soundtrack.

    Show how the film or programme makers construct this mood and go on to explain how it influences your appreciation of the text as a whole.

    You must refer to specific examples and to at least two of the following: mood, soundtrack, mise-en-scène, editing, or any other appropriate feature.

18. Choose a film where the makers challenge certain conventions of a particular genre such as Western, Horror, Science Fiction, Film Noir.

    Show how the film makers challenge these conventions and go on to explain how this approach affects your appreciation of the genre.

    You must refer to specific examples and to at least two of the following: genre, theme, characterisation, plot, or any other appropriate feature.

19. Choose a film or *TV drama in which the past plays a crucial role.

    Show how the film or programme makers reveal the significance of the past and why it is important to your appreciation of key elements of the text.

    You must refer to specific examples and to at least two of the following: editing, mise-en-scène, plot, character, or any other appropriate feature.

*"TV drama" includes a single play, a series or a serial.

SECTION E—LANGUAGE

20. Consider the spoken language of a particular generation—young children, teenagers, an older generation, for example.

    Identify what you consider to be the particular aspects of language which typify this group, and show to what extent these aspects of language operate to the benefit of the generation to which they belong.

    You must refer to specific examples and to at least two of the following language concepts: vocabulary, grammar, dialect, accent, or any other appropriate concept.

21. Consider the language used to communicate with the general public in specialist areas such as legal, financial, medical, or government services.

    Identify the areas of difficulty in such communications and show to what extent the provider of any of these services has succeeded in overcoming these difficulties.

    You must refer to specific examples and to at least two of the following language concepts: vocabulary, register, jargon, sentence structure, or any other appropriate concept.

22. Consider any form of Scots, either written or spoken, with which you are familiar.

    To what extent are the users of your chosen form of Scots advantaged or disadvantaged?

    You must refer to specific examples and to at least two of the following language concepts: vocabulary, grammar, accent, tone, or any other appropriate concept.

23. Consider the contribution made to English by the language of other parts of the world during the last 100 years or so—for example, the languages of the Indian Sub-Continent, the USA, Continental Europe, the Caribbean . . .

    By identifying contributions made to English, discuss to what extent it gains from its ability to "borrow" words, phrases and idioms from other languages.

    You must refer to specific examples and to at least two of the following language concepts: vocabulary, slang, idiom, grammar, or any other appropriate concept.

[END OF QUESTION PAPER]

[BLANK PAGE]